MW01514597

Whoa Dammit!

My Life as an Outfitter

As told by Duane Neal

Black Otter Guide Service
Pray, Montana

Compiled and edited by
Sonya Neal

Copyright 2020 by Sonya Neal

All rights reserved

Contents

About the Author

Duane was born January 21, 1936 to Archie and Cleo Neal at home on the family ranch in McPherson County, Nebraska. He was the oldest of ten children and grew up riding horses and working Hereford cattle in the Sandhills.

He graduated from Tryon High School, Nebraska in 1953. He joined the Air Force in 1955 and proudly served his nation for four years, being the first soldier in his family.

Duane married the love of his life, Ruth Hyatt, on September 30, 1961 and have celebrated many of their anniversaries in the high mountains.

They often explored new country by themselves, always wanting to see what was on the other side of the mountain.

The couple moved to White Sulphur Springs, Montana in 1962 to work on a cattle ranch. In September of that same year they bought a ranch in Paradise Valley where they raised a family.

In 1968 Duane and Ruth bought the Black Otter Guide Service, "Where you come as strangers and leave as friends." Their three daughters, Shelly, Sonya, and Shawna were always very much a part of the business.

Duane was known as the Head-Gahoona of the outfit and made many lifelong friends in that role.

He enjoyed leatherworking and made many of the outfit's saddles and tack; every family member had a pair of his chaps, much to their delight!

He rode a lot of good horses and loved a well-behaved mule string. He was proud of his packing and some said he could "pack anything with hair on it."

He would record his memoirs on tape while riding down the trail and many of these recordings are colorfully punctuated by "whoa dammit" when his mule string didn't behave.

Duane was instrumental in the formation of the Montana Outfitters and Guides Association and served as their President, he was also President of the Treasure State Outfitters. In 1981 he traveled to Washington, D.C. to lobby against a bill which would have allowed for Forest Service permits to be sold to the highest bidder.

The photos are a mix of new and old from family albums, an assortment of random pictures to include the grandkids and fit the tale. It was a joy compiling this book as it brought back lots of fond memories as well as gifting me with new ones.

I hope you enjoy and treasure this memento of an authentic cowboy, my dad.

~Sonya Neal, editor

Black Otter Guide Service

This is the beginning of our 30th year outfitting in the Absaroka Beartooth Wilderness, Yellowstone National Park, and the Gallatin National Forest. We start our season the first part of July and pack in summer trips until early September after which we guide hunters until late November.

I'm Duane Neal. My wife, Ruth, and I and our family have run the Black Otter Guide Service since 1968.

It all began in Cooke City....

Cooke City, the One-Street Town

Shawna, Sonya & Pinto

Cooke City is a small recreational mountain town just barely on the map. It's the northeast entrance to Yellowstone Park. We spent five years in Cooke City in the summertime. We gave horseback rides and took pack trips, ran a motel, and had a filling station; anything to make a dollar. When a car drove in I usually washed the windshields.

Our oldest daughter was about six years old and decided she'd make a dollar, too. One day her and her sister got an egg crate and got up and washed the windshields, so somebody gave them a 50-cent piece. After that a car couldn't even come to a screeching halt and they were out there washing the windshield.

When they wasn't making enough money with us they went up the street to the general store and talked to Betty Bishop and asked her if she had a job for them and she give them a job. They come back and told their mother they could only work for her until noon and then they had to go up and work at the store.

A friend of ours came and saw me one day and says, "I've got to get rid of my horses. They're out on the Forest Service and my dad's going to shoot them or send them to the can if I don't do something. Can I give them to you?"

I says, "Well, we'll take them if we can use them."

He says, "That's fine, I do want that one black back someday if I ever get around to it."

Seems like he had five head. One was a black three- or four-year-old colt, heck of a horse, a gelding. I kind of made him my private horse. Then there was another black gelding and a palomino mare and a big bay gelding. We made good use of those horses for quite a few years until finally Walt came and got the one we called Little Walt and took him home.

Another one was a little Shetland that came up about halfway to your belt or something like that and had a little two-wheel pony cart and harness that went with it.

One day I came off a pack trip and saw the pony and the

cart hooked up to the hitching rack. I says, "What's going on?"
Ruth told me to "just wait and see." Pretty quick here comes
some kid wanting to pay Shelly to take him around the block. I
found out she's charging them 50 cents to go around the block in
the pony cart. I guess she thought she ought to be making
money, too. She had a pretty good business lined up there. So
Shelly learned how to make money in a hurry.

That pony, if you had it in with your horses you couldn't
catch it, it would run underneath the bellies of your horses and
stuff like that. You had to have it hog-tied to the fence to keep it
home rather than at the neighbors. I finally had to sell it.

4

We had a hitching rack across from the motel we were running in Cooke City. Next to it was an old log cabin that supposedly some judge had lived in. Some wrangler several years before us had put a big sign on it that read cabin for rent, air-conditioned, 50 cents. It was pretty well air-conditioned as it didn't have a roof, no windows or doors, holes with no chinking.

Anyway, that drew a lot of attention and helped us a lot on our hourly rides. The gal that owned the property didn't think it was too great though so finally she moved a better-looking cabin in down there. That didn't help us so much.

Shawna & Dixie

Chinook

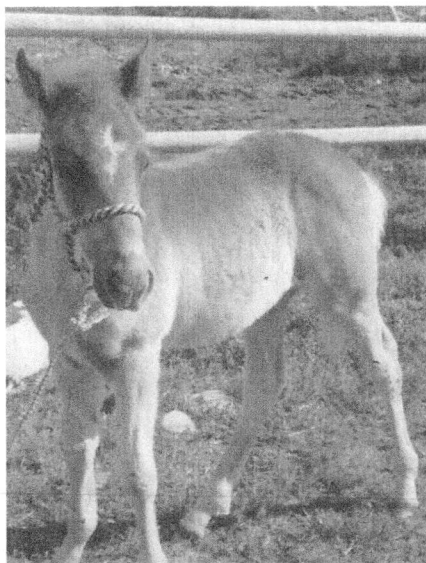

Another big attraction we had in addition to the hourly rides was one year we had a mare give birth to a little colt and a couple of days later the mare died from a twisted intestine or something, so we raised the colt on a bottle. The kids fed the colt and named him Chinook as it was born during a chinook. We lived in Cooke City and kept it by the Anvil Inn.

They would bring it down to the hitching rack at the Rawhide where we had our horses. Of course, every little kid that went through town in the car had to get their parents to stop so they could pet the colt. "Can we have a picture with our kid?"

"50 cents." That led to an hourly ride on horseback. Helped us quite a little. The guests at the Anvil Inn would bring leftover roasting ears off their plates and everything else to feed the colt. You can't believe what that colt learned to eat.

That fall after we got back to Pray the colt was running around in the yard. Ruth was cooking supper one night for some company and had the table all set. The door was open because it was pretty warm. Lo and behold she looked around and here's the colt in the kitchen where the table was with its nose in the dinner plate. Of course, she wasn't too happy and ran him out.

We had a hunter from Pennsylvania who showed up with a camper on the pickup that his wife was going to stay in while he was up hunting. The first night she about had a heart attack, thought the world was coming to an end or something, for that colt got under that camper and it was just the right height to scratch his back. He'd get to rubbing, the camper would get to rocking, and she thought we were having an earthquake.

One of the first times I ever had Chinook on a pack trip was back in Hellroaring. I decided there weren't any fish in Grizzly Creek so I was going to transplant a few out of the lake So when we caught enough fish I just dumped them in the five-gallon jerry cans and put one on each side of Chinook. He took about three steps, the water sloshed, and he started bucking.

People from Hawaii were with me and one guy, Bob, was a commercial artist for the newspaper. There's a watercolor on my stairway that Bob painted right after that and gave to me showing the fish going high and the fish going low.

The colt finally grew up. We broke him to pack and then to ride and he's packed a lot of kids around the mountains. Finally sold him to a friend of ours, for he's a good gentle little horse.

Tanner Ellis & Chinook

Cowboys, Guns, and the Local Law

Alvin Pierce

One night some cowboys came to town from somewhere and they proceeded to shoot up the Range Rider's Lodge in Silver Gate. The owner talked to a few people, word spread, and so lo and behold, the citizens of Cooke City and Silver Gate all showed up at the Range Rider's that night.

Arrowhead Ranch Branding Crew (Pierces)

Basically all we did was stand around with our hands in our pockets and, of course, each one of us had a .38 in our belt or something a little bigger.

So the guys that raised hell the night before were good little boys.

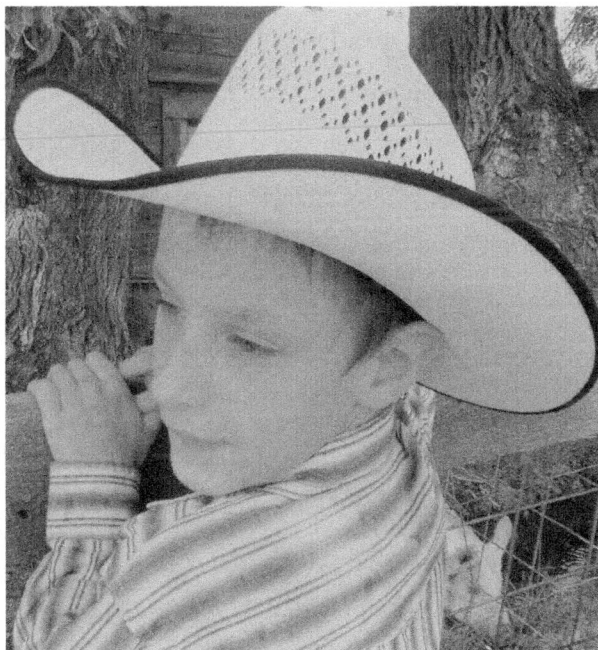

Marshall Pierce

They got out of town without a big squawk. It could have got kind of serious.

A Good Idea at the Time

When we were getting ready to move back to Pray from Cooke City one summer we decided well, we'll take the horses across the mountains instead of trucking them and have a little leisurely trip by ourselves, just us, the family and the guide.

We got packed up down at Cooke City and it was a real nice hot day. We headed up over Daisy Pass and were planning to make Bob Hart's camp down on Lake Creek before dark. We got on top of Daisy out in the open and it decided it was going to start raining, then it started snowing and hailing. We were all out in the open and got soaked before we could get our coats on.

We headed down toward Lake Abundance. I decided as miserable as it was getting and as much trouble as we were having maybe we better just stop right there and unpack and go back in the morning and truck the horses around, like we should have done to start with. Lake Abundance people have been driving down there for years and years and have cut every piece of wood that resembles firewood within half a mile of the lake. We tried to get a fire started and never did get much more than a smudge.

There was a pickup sitting there so I decided I would get me some fire starter. I dropped a rope down the gas tank and

11

pulled it up. That wouldn't even burn, at least not enough to get a good fire started. I looked all over for some dry wood but never did get a decent fire started. I finally got some tents up, jerked the clothes off the kids and rubbed them down good so we could get them warmed up, fed them hot Tang, and stuck them in their sleeping bags.

We got the mules unpacked and turned everything loose. Some of them wanted to go down Slough Creek, some of them went the other way, but we got the ones going down Slough Creek turned around. The next morning we looked around and we had some horses and mules but some were gone.

So I headed Ruth and the girls and the guide back to Cooke City with what we had. We didn't even pick up the gear, we figured we'd come back in the pickup and get that. Then I went looking for the other horses, found them and got them headed back over Daisy Pass. Just got on top and here came Jim Langston with his pickup, the guy I tried to steal some gas from the night before.

He asked, "Do you want a ride?"

I says, "Heck yeah."

I tied my bridle reins of my horse up, slapped him on the butt and let him go after the others and jumped in the pickup.

12

I guess when my horse came into town it kind of upset the girls. They thought Daddy had been hurt or something.

I made it in one piece though.

We got in our pickup and went back to Lake Abundance and got all our gear and hauled it back to Pray. Got the big truck and hauled the horses back over to Pray like we should have done in the first place. The storm only lasted about a day and then it was nice from then on. We would have been okay going on. But it sure took the fun out of it right off the start.

Shawna was just a baby and had the common sense to stay with Grandma while we came across the hills.

Scrambled Eggs

One year when we were up at Cooke City I sent the hired man down to Pray after mules, and Ruth went along to get some groceries and a few things. They didn't get back to Cooke City until about 2:00 in the morning so I was pretty worried.

The next morning I found out they only brought back about half the stuff they went after, they just left two mules. That meant that Ruth and I had to go back about a week later and get those two mules. So we did a whole bunch of shopping, got about 60 dozen eggs and some other groceries we were going to need in the next few days.

Then we stopped at the horse pasture and caught the mules. I'm going to have to admit those mules were a little bit hard to catch for there was a pretty big catch pen there. But we got them caught. I had a little two-horse trailer that was made down in Arizona for three-quarter-size horses, I guess, or something. Anyway, it was only about three-quarters as big as most horse trailers and it had an open top.

The mules, Francis and Sassafras, the first thing they did was try to jump out of the horse trailer. So I tied their noses down solid to the horse trailer and we headed for Cooke City. We got about five miles from Cooke City. I was tooling along

14

about 50 miles an hour and I hear kerthump in the back end.

"What was that?"

Ruth looked out the back window and says, "You've got a mule in the back of the pickup."

"Impossible," I says but I stopped anyway to check. Sure enough, I have a mule in the back of the pickup upside down with all four feet sticking in the air with its nose tied to the horse trailer. Well, what do I do now? I didn't want to cut the halter rope too bad. Finally I worked it loose and the mule fell out of the back of the pickup. I noticed something is running down the pavement.

"What's that?" I figured it was probably the blood and guts from the mule or something like that.

Ruth says, "Dear, that's the eggs."

It's getting along about midnight about now. That mule wouldn't go in the horse trailer. I worked, and worked, and finally I say to heck with it so I tied the mule to the back of the horse trailer and headed for Cooke City. We're doing fine with the mule motating along behind me. We came to a little town that's known as Silver Gate, Montana, home of the Range Rider's Lodge that has a band every Saturday night. Everybody we know is there.

Ruth says, "Dear, are you going to lead that mule past the Range Rider's?"

"No, you've got a point there."

So I stopped and we got the mule loaded; she had a little more incentive now. We drove past the Range Rider's with two mules in the horse trailer like they're supposed to be, to Cooke City. I started to unload the mules and the one mule jumped right out of the horse trailer, he'd had enough of that thing. Not Francis, you couldn't get her out.

I'd had all I wanted with that mule for one day, so to heck with you, if you want to stay in the trailer, you can stay in the trailer. I shut the gate and went to bed. I went down the next morning and opened the gate. Francis backed right out of the horse trailer like a well-broken mule.

So we unloaded the groceries, including what is left of the eggs, up at the house. We saved about 29 dozen eggs out of that fiasco, which wasn't bad considering that mule lit right on top of them.

Let's Hit the Trail!

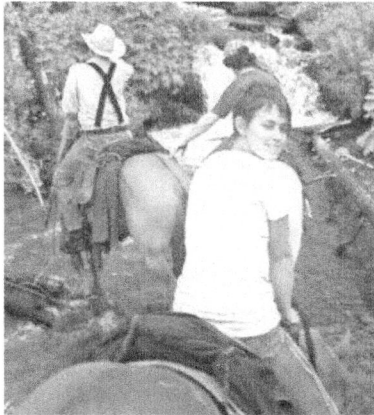

Duane, Luke & Lea

An interesting trip we took was the Appaloosa Horse Club with 200 Appaloosa horses. Guests furnished their own horse but we did the packing.

Shelly & Sonya

The Langford, Washburn, Doan expedition explored Yellowstone Park in 1870, and 113 years later we retraced a portion of that route with some descendants of Langford. We found a few of the original campsites on the south and east end of the lake.

Sonya & Lea Christiansen

We went into Surprise Creek, a very remote area. We figured Everett's got lost on the way to Surprise Creek and were lost for 30 days. We found a campsite where ax marks still visible on the larger trees were probably made by the expedition.

Bailey Francis

We have 11 mules and 15 horses on this trip. A lot of summer trips that we've been taking have had as high as 22 guests. Some of them have been moving trips, others have been into a base camp where we've stayed.

Shelly Francis

19

Wildfire Cookin'

Marshall & Mariah Pierce

The fires of 1988 singed probably 90 percent of all the ground that we've covered since our Grizzly Creek camp about six days ago. Lost Creek had a really hot burn, it killed practically everything in the bottom of the creek. There are a few green trees on the ridge on the left side of Lost Creek but it's also a lot of dead burned stuff

We tried to get on packing for the fires of 1988 when they first started but we had one more summer pack trip and I told them I'd like to wait until I got through with that to start. By the time I got through with that pack trip they had all the packers they wanted hired.

Later on they had us bid on rehab contract in Hellroaring drainage. They didn't tell us a whole heck of a lot about where it was going to be, or how we were going to get there, or anything like that, they just wanted us to feed so many people in the backcountry setting. It was going to be 18-19 miles into camp. So we bid it accordingly, and I'll be darned if we didn't get it.

Well, we still didn't know what was going to take place too well or anything else, or how we'd get there. One morning they called us up and says, "Be at the helipad at Gardiner at 7:00 the next morning." So we were up there with three pickup loads of gear, food, four or five help, and what have you and unloaded the stuff. They told us, "You're going to have to pick out a campsite near where the Bull Moose cabin was."

"I better go on the first helicopter then." So I jumped in the first helicopter and we flew back there. They let me off at Teddy's camp and I started hiking up toward Bull Moose. Got a fair site picked out where there were half a dozen green trees. Lo and behold, here comes the first chopper load of gear. I pointed out a tree for him to drop it and he went back. By 1:00 the crew was coming in, by 4:00 we had five wall tents going up in the air and the cots in. The cook was kind of standing around with his hands in his pocket, taking it all in. By 7:00 that night we fed 25 people a meal undercover on seats and tables.

Now if we'd done that with a pack string we'd been at the very minimum one full day getting in there. We probably had 20 packhorse loads of stuff. We'd have been another day setting up, for sure. When that crew come in at 1:00 they started cutting firewood for us. Boy, I'll tell you what, it didn't take them very long to lay in a supply of wood. There were 25 of them, a couple three guys on saws were sawing, the rest were packing it to the cook tent, and some were splitting it. They put in a lot of wood in short order.

Hot Boots

You've probably heard about cowboys roping something and sliding across the corral on the end their rope? I had to pack a group out of the Beartooths one time and Ruth had just brought me a pair of boots with brand new half soles home from town the night before. So I stuck them on and I rode up to the camp and I packed up. I had five mules then, they were all black mules, and they all knew where they belonged in the string. I had these mules tied to trees around the camp as they weren't nice gentle mules that you could just drop their lead rope and go to packing. I got all the mules packed and started stringing them up.

The lead mule was tied to a tree, then came Francis with Sassafras behind her and then Rosie which left Rufus last and he was way across the clearing on the other side of the camp. I untied him and he turned and I thought he was going to town, so I set in the air and he slid me across the clearing to the back of the pack string and stopped.

Well, I couldn't get them boots off fast enough for they had really heated up sliding on the granite gravel that covered the campsite. When they finally cooled off enough so I could get them back on I rode to town and when I took them off they both had holes through those new half soles. Had to send them back to the big city to get a new pair of half soles on them. That's probably the fastest I ever went through half soles in my life.

Check Your Cinch

One time I left my brother Keith and the cook in Big Creek for two or three days. I had to go out for some reason, I don't know why. I rode over to camp and nobody came out of the tent so I got off my horse and walked in and here's the cook and here is Keith sitting there with big old bumps on his head and eyes swelled shut.

I says, "What happened to you?"

Finally he says, "Well, I was looking for the horses and went down in the creek."

Keith always rode with his cinch loose under his horse's belly. When the horse stuck his head in the creek to get a drink of water Keith and the saddle and bridle and everything else went off the over the horse's head. I'm not sure whether Keith ever found his glasses or not but he sure took a lot of bumps.

He was trying to get thawed out when I got there.

Grizzly Creek Campfire & Pika

Don't Use the Cook's Water!

Anita Kuntz, Ruth's sister

The Wilderness Society always sent a doctor on their trips. One year the doctor brought his wife. The first camp was at Grizzly Creek. The cook was heating up water to do the dishes and when she went to get her water and the doctor's wife had used it all to take a bath. Didn't make the cook very happy, in fact she was damned unhappy.

The next day when they packed up and moved to Buffalo Fork, where is the doctor's duffel? For some reason it got left behind at Grizzly Creek. I don't think it was intentional but the doctor and his wife sure thought it was. They had it hid up in the trees so I don't know for sure what happened.

Anyway, Shelly and one of the guides got on their horses the next morning and rode back to Grizzly Creek and got that duffel. Only made about a 32-mile ride out of it.

Still didn't mollify the doctor's wife much but she didn't use the cook's water anymore.

Marshall

Cold-Water Bathing

One time we had a couple from somewhere back East that we brought in to camp. When the girls were cooking supper they would cook in their swimsuits and then go out and jump in a big pool in the creek. The guys would be fishing at the lower end of it pulling fish out. This guy from back East thought, boy, that looks good, as his back was hurting. He jumped in and then crawled back to his tent when he came out. He wasn't outside the tent for two days until the night before we were going to move.

I told him, "I'm going down to get a helicopter to get you out of here."

He was planning on riding but we got a helicopter and got him out of there. He spent about 15 days in the hospital in Livingston. What had happened was on the way up here he had one of those two-wheel baggage trailers they pull behind cars, a little utility trailer. They got a flat tire so instead of putting the jack under it he thought he'd just lift it up to change the tire and he strained his back. When he jumped in that cold water that's all it took, it tightened up just like that. Pinched nerve or something.

Leave the cold-water bathing to the girls.

Cold-Water Sitting

We had a gal on a summer trip a year or two in the Absarokas and then she booked a trip into Big Creek, wanted to see a little different country. Unbeknownst to me, she had to sit in cold water every morning. I'm not sure why. I put her in the camp up Bark Cabin and the water wasn't deep enough so the guide moved her over to Big Creek Meadows where there were some deep pools.

In the Second World War she had stood all night in the river with water up to her chin trying to evade the Germans, which she did, so I guess that had something to do with this peculiarity.

Stuck Horse

We camped on Broad Creek in Yellowstone one time and one day we went down to some hot springs, riding down a long meadow to get there. Spotting a trail on the other side of the meadow I says, "Hey, Murphy, here's a good crossing right here, why don't we go across here?"

The buffalo had been going across there it looked like, as one of the guys found a buffalo skull. No reason horses couldn't cross in the same place. Ol' Murphy who was leading the way started down there and got to the creek which was about 10 to 12 feet wide right at the crossing and probably six inches deep. Murphy started to put his horse in but he was riding an old Appy that absolutely refused to go where he could get in trouble. That should have been a hint.

I told Murphy "Why don't you move over and I'll try."

Of course, my horse didn't want to go either so I jammed the spurs and reins to him and he lit in the middle of the creek and started down and down and down. Finally, he started trying to paddle for the other shore but he couldn't get out. So he flipped over and just about upside downed on top of me and headed back for the shore we started from. We got over there and he got his nose out on terra firma and he stopped. I'm still half a horse length from home so I got out of the saddle and up on top of the horse. Murphy stuck out his hand and I walked the horse's neck until I could get up on terra firma myself.

Well, we sat there debating on what to do and how to get that horse out and let him rest a little while. Finally, he got rested up so we all gave a heave on him the best we could and he came up out of there, none the worse for the wear.

Holey Pants

I'll tell you about Ruth's holey pants. Might have to change the name.

When the dudes went out of Broad Creek I left the camp in and had Ruth come up and we went in for a couple of nights, then over the top into Crystal Creek. The day we were in there I told Ruth, "Let's ride down to these hot springs."

Okay. We went down to the hot springs and looked around and we set down along the hot spring and ate our lunch. Then we got on our horses and went back home to the camp. When we got to camp Ruth begins busily preparing supper.

She turned around with her rear towards me and I says, "Why did you wear worn-out Levis?"

They looked brand new except for right in the seat of

her pants. There were some good holes there, about the size of a dinner plate, two of them.

She says, "These aren't worn out."

"Well," I says, "you better go in the tent and take a look." She did. So much for her new Levis.

The ground had been a little wet there where she had sat a little closer to the sulfur springs and the chlorine in the ground soaked up into her pants and ate her pants up. I was over far enough that I didn't get any of it, I guess. My Levis didn't get holes in them, anyway.

Mountain Sledding

Another kind of hairy situation I got into is one spring I brought a bunch of kids into Grizzly Creek on a youth trip, the first pack out of the box. I believe we came in June that year. We came through Jardine and Yellowstone Park. When we got to Grizzly Creek we decided one day we'll ride up to the pass and see how the snow is on the other side and how soon we can get over it.

We got up there and ate lunch. When we got through eating I thought I'd meander down the other side and see how it is. I was walking a big old snow field there that went down and off the end of it was a good cliff quite a ways down. I was walking along there doing okay, digging the sides of my shoes in, and suddenly my feet slipped out from under me. I started sliding down that snowdrift.

I look and see there's one chance of stopping from going over the edge there and that's to get to that tree out there about a third of the way down. I was kind of headed right for it but had to do a little steering to get to that direction. I did make the tree, or part of the branch, and it held and stopped me. I got the heck off of that thing.

I would have probably got stopped down at the bottom somewhere before I went over the edge, I don't know. I never did go on down and look to see how far that snow went out before it dropped over the edge. I think I probably would have been able to get stopped. That was a little bit scary.

Not for the Faint of Heart

One thing that's scary as far as water goes is fording Slough Creek in high water. I don't swim much better than a rock and you go out across there and the water's up to about a horse's neck or something like that. It makes you wonder whether he's going to stay up or whether you're going to be able to get to the other side. We've always made it though.

There's also the swinging bridge across the Yellowstone River at the gravel pit.

That's what we have to cross if we come in from Yellowstone Park to Grizzly Creek.

I don't know how high it is or how long it is, but I always say about 300 foot high and 300 foot long. It sure looks like it. There's a steel plate on each end of it. If your horse had never been on there you have a hell of a time getting your horse to step out across there. If your lead horse has been on that bridge before generally he'll take off across and anything behind him will follow. You get to about the middle and you got about eight or ten head horses on it and it gets to bouncing pretty good, swaying, and you kind of wonder what's going on. Finally you have to stop your packhorse and break the cadence on the darn thing so it will settle down. It gets a little scary. There's one consolation, as far as I know, nobody's ever went off of it. I know of one guy whose horse was supposed to have stepped through it though.

Mass

Another great guy we had on trips for several years was Father Mark Fitzgerald who was a Jesuit priest, taught at Notre Dame. I'm not sure how many years he went with us but he went a lot. He always had mass the first Friday night of the trip and it usually wound up being at Buffalo Fork.

Slough Creek

Alvin & Mariah

We're back at our Slough Creek camp. Over the years we've seen quite a few grizzly bears, moose, black bears, and a few elk here.

We came in through the park with Chip Risotto's group of five brothers and a wife. Spent two nights in 2S8 down in Yellowstone Park to fish, moved up here yesterday, will spend four nights here. Horses here in Slough Creek sure don't want to stay anywhere you camp.

Down at 2S8 the first night they took off just about the time to gather them just before dark. I took off after them and finally caught them crossing Slough Creek on Frenchy's Meadow north of the Lost Creek camp. That must be five miles from the Slough Creek camp. There are two gates down there at the Silver Tip and both of them were open so they went right on through. I caught a bunch of them, tailed them up and headed back for camp. Got in about midnight.

But the loose horses or mules that I couldn't tail up wouldn't follow me. They wound up in the Ranger Station. The next morning when the Silver Tip came to wrangle they caught them at the Ranger Station and just shut the gate. So I had them. Took me a day and half to get everything gathered back up.

The next night I kept about two thirds of the horses tied up. I'll be darned if the ones I didn't have tied I couldn't find the next morning. I rode for a couple hours and finally found them right across the creek from camp. I don't know where they'd been. While I was out looking they wandered in. That made me feel a little better.

We got in here about 2:00 yesterday afternoon. This morning we got up at 6:00 and went to get the horses. I stopped at a couple of camps along the way and tarried a little bit too long. I'll be darned if the horses weren't halfway to Lake Abundance on the Lake Creek trail up in an old site that we have camped at before. I caught them just about the time they made it there. We came back in a bigger hurry than they went up.

This is a pretty good bunch of fishermen but like all fishermen they have trouble making up their mind what they want to do, other than fish.

Luke Christiansen

39

Horses, Mules, and Other Critters

Luke

I've had quite a few mules over the years, even raised a couple of them. One of them turned out to be pretty good. The other one was kind of a snaky son-of-a-gun. We finally got rid of him. The other mule was a black mule. We wound up with five black mules eventually. We had one sorrel mule. Another friend of ours, he called me up one day and he says, "I got these five mules down here, two of them are ones you used last summer and three are mates to them."

He wanted to sell them and had a pretty good price on the bunch so we bought them. We wound up with 12 mules. The others are all pretty good mules. You have to watch any mule, you know, they've got their own way of doing things. Once you get a pack on them they pack all day and never touch a tree.

40

We had a set of mules we got from Morris Blakely; Pat, Sassafras, Rufus, Rosy, and Francis. Had to think for a little bit on them. They all had their own special characteristics.

Sassafras was a snaky little son-of-a- gun. You wanted to watch her. I didn't once. Would usually tie her up with her lips tied to the hitching post or something so she couldn't get much room. I forgot to do that and I was loading some sacks of elk quarters on her. Went to drag one around her and I forgot that she was loose. She kicked me twice with both hind feet before I could lay down.

Stretched all the ligaments in my left leg pretty bad and I couldn't navigate too well for a while. Eventually I had to have it replaced a couple of years ago.

41

That was a heck of a good mule if you ever got a pack on her. She'd never touch a tree. That whole string was that way.

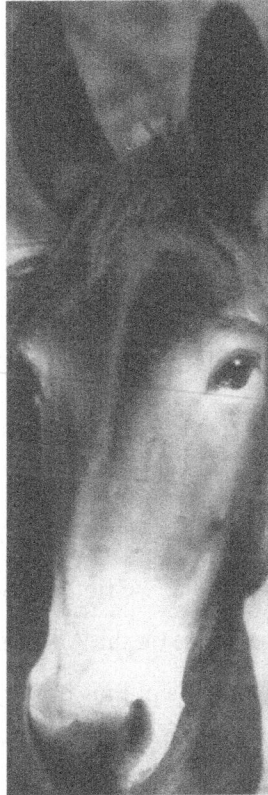

Ol' Rufus, he got a bunch of cancer. Finally shot him. I took him back in Grizzly Creek where he spent most of his life and left him there. Ol' Pat, she got struck by lightning. Sassafras and Francis and Rosy died natural deaths, I guess.

Jack

We had one mule we got with the outfit. His name was Jack. He was about 37 years old, we figured, when he finally met his maker. There's a picture on the Antler's Bar in Columbus when he's two years old and he's pulling a pony cart. That mule, in our Grizzly Creek camp, would take the horses all over Hellroaring. But he would bring them home twice a day for their pellets. That was a pretty cheap wrangler.

Jack got very sick one time, I'm not sure just what his problem was. But when we left the Slough creek camp I got as far as the Bull Creek trail and he just couldn't hack it so I turned

43

him loose. I was going to be back in here a couple weeks anyway. Hung his packsaddle up in the tree and left old Jack.

When we came back in a couple weeks sure enough he's all well and ready to go again. The packsaddle didn't fare so well, the porcupines or something got to it and ate about half of it up. I guess while we were gone he went clear to the Silver Tip and clear back up to Bull Creek about every day looking for us.

That was Jack.

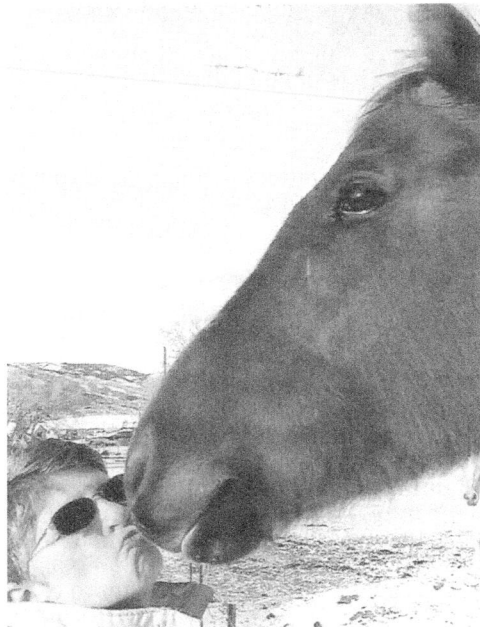

Shawna Pierce

Scrooge

Bailey

I bought a brown mule one time from a friend of ours. He had worked at Silver Tip Ranch on Slough Creek, packed in that area. Well, this brown mule we called Scrooge. Every time we camped on Slough Creek he always wound up in Silver Tip's corral when they wrangled their horses in the morning. I guess he thought that was still home.

I went down to get him one morning. He was standing alongside a fence that was about a foot and a half above his back when I started across the corral with his halter to catch him. I looked at him and he was standing along this side of the fence, on my side of the fence. Now I've seen mules and horses jump, but the Silver Tip corral must have been 5½ to 6 feet tall.

I looked down at the ground and looked back up at the mule. Well, the damn fence was between me and the mule. He apparently had jumped it flatfooted and hadn't even broke a sweat. Took him about ten years to get over thinking he belonged to the Silver Tip. I guess he couldn't read.

We've had lots of horses over the years. Used to be up in Cooke City, when we spent the summers there, we run about 70 head of horses between the hourly rides, day trips, and pack trips. Now we run about 35 or 40, counting the mules.

Shelly & Shawnee

46

Goblin

Had a horse I named Goblin. He was named right, for he spooked at about everything that came along. He was pretty tall.

One time down in Yellowstone Park I tied him to the bumper of the pickup which was tied to the horse trailer. But I didn't think a sack might blow past Goblin. Well, one did and Goblin went backwards pulling the horse trailer and the pickup. Somebody had to jump in and set the brake and then he couldn't go any farther. He didn't like a rope under his tail either, that would make him buck pretty good. In fact, Ruth got bucked off that way one time.

We were packing camp out one year and we got about halfway down the trail to home. There was a chunk of wood

47

about two feet long and six inches wide and a couple inches thick laying alongside the trail. It was white and weathered. It hadn't been there but for 452 years. But Goblin had a problem every time he come past that chunk of wood. Instead of getting off and throwing it out of the way so he couldn't see it I thought he'll get over it before the end of the season. When we went to pack out he still wasn't over it. This was right in the middle of a slide rock hillside.

So we come down there and here is that piece of wood and Goblin is blowing and smoking. I get him past it and we get down the trail about three steps and my mule decides he's going to wipe his nose on Goblin's tail or something. He did that and Goblin jumped about 30 feet, caught me off balance and I went off to the right. I got my right foot in the stirrup, my left spur happened to catch the cantle of the saddle or I would have been long gone.

After that first jump I saw a tree coming on the lower edge of the trail. I couldn't reach the saddle horn but I could pull on the reins, I still had them. I pulled Goblin and made him hit that tree so I could push myself back in the saddle. I got sat back down and said "I guess I'm ready."

Gary says, "Well where is your hat?"

48

I look around, my hat is halfway down Big Creek on that hillside. So I got off my horse and started down there. It had been wet and it was slick, didn't have much problem getting down there, for I slid all the way. But when I started back up, every step I'd take I'll lose about three backward. But I did eventually get back up to Goblin , with my hat.

Another time I was coming off of Wallace with Goblin and when I come over the edge I look down the trail and there was two guys coming up the trail. I looked again and there were two guys and a white spot and they aren't moving. So I go a little ways farther and looked down and here are two guys and the white spot has disappeared. That went on about every couple hundred feet. When I looked, there was something different. I got down to the same switchback those guys were on and there was only two guys. No, there's a white spot. Goblin pretty near went back up over Wallace.

These guys had a young burro that they just were breaking, first trip out. Apparently the burro thought it was being overworked and so every time they'd put about a 20-pound pack on his back he would lay down. They'd take it off and he would jump up. That was what the white spot was/no white spot.

Goblin turned around raising hell and I couldn't get him

any closer and I was having a heck of a time even keeping him that close. Eventually I just cut across the switchback and went on down the trail. For the rest of that year and part of the next year every time we come to that spot Goblin would have a fit.

On another trip we got on down the trail pretty near to Count's Meadow and Goblin stopped and he's looking. I'm looking and I can't see anything that he should be concerned about. Pretty quick I see something white behind a tree.

I yelled, "Is somebody back there?"

"Yes," I said, "Step out here where I can see you and say something so my horse knows what you are." So they did and Goblin settled down a little bit. They were backpacking and they had bought some whitetail deerskins and had them rolled up on top of their backpack which spooked my trusty steed.

Deadman

A friend called me up and he says, "Hey, bring your truck down here". So I took my truck down and we went out east of Livingston a ways, backed up to the loading chute. We run a bunch of horses in. We get back to Livingston, my friend says, "I want this one and this one, you might as well take the rest of them out there to see what you can use, all they need is a little riding."

That's the kind of thing most people tell us, "All they need is a little riding." Well, some of them need a little riding, but some of them need a lot.

So anyway, one of them I took home was a big stud about six years old, seven, I don't know. The first thing we did was make a gelding out of him. When he healed up we took him to Cooke City, threw a sawbuck packsaddle on him and 100 pounds of salt in each side. Then we tied the packsacks down to the sawbuck so they wouldn't come off, but we left them so they'd flop.

We cut that son-of-a-gun loose and come out of the barn with me in the lead and Jack riding drag. That son-of-a-gun went in the air, come down, the salt stayed in the air for a second and then it come down. When it come down, they just about met in the middle.

That horse, he went oomph and that was the last jump he ever made that I know of. We packed him for two or three years. He was always looking at you, acting like he might want to eat you, but he never did.

I finally got cold feet and sold the son-of-a-gun. Took him to Billings to the horse sale with his shoes still on.

Well, when we turned him in the ring, he gave out a couple of snorts, the auctioneer says, "Miles City, here we come!" (Miles City Bucking Horse Sale.) Well, the horse about topped the sale that day. I don't know if he ever bucked out of a bucking chute or not but I think he did.

We named him Deadman.

Paint

We had a little black paint colt that wasn't very big. The wranglers got to letting him buck a little so they could impress the girls. The only problem was it got so the horse was impressing the girls more than the wranglers were.

Finally we decided, well we'll just sell that son of a gun, he might as well be eating somebody else's grass. They had a bucking horse sale over in Bozeman. When that paint come out of the chute gate, him and his rider parted company in a hurry. Now he didn't make too much of a bucking horse I don't think. He was pretty small and wasn't very high-end at that sale but he sure unloaded that guy.

Frenchie

Had another horse we called Frenchie we bought somewhere along the line, maybe down at Colorado, a little Indian pony. That son-of-a-gun, the wranglers they'd get real brave and use him to wrangle with, jump on him at the corral or wherever it happened to be and, of course, he'd have to show off to the dudes. So they took the spurs to him, generally made about three jumps. Frenchie would unpile them, unload them, stop right dead still as soon as his reins touched the ground.

"Well, come on you wise son-of-a-gun, get back on and try me again." If they got back on they'd take it a little easy and break him out slow.

Pokey

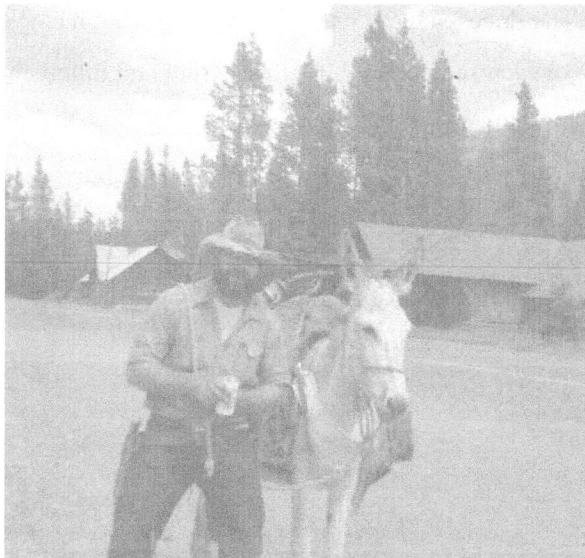

John Newbauer

A friend of ours give us a burro one time to use. We thought that was a blessing. We had a lot of people that summer and needed everything with four legs that we could find. Now that burro was a good burro, packed 30 pounds, or 30 loaves of bread I think is what I put on that burro, if I remember right.

The dudes would take off for camp before us cowboys on moving days, then we'd pack up and generally pass them at lunchtime. Well, I've got this burro on the tail end of my string and of course my saddle horse walks twice as fast as the burro wants to walk. So we get to where the dudes are and the burro lays down. The dudes want to pack his load and what have you. Some of them even seemed to think I was cruel and inhumane for making him all sweaty and tired.

So needless to say, I got rid of Pokey. That burro would've been fine had he been walking along at his own pace but when you put him on a lead rope and he had to keep up, he just couldn't do it.

Sarge

Gary Francis

Probably one of the most dangerous situations I've been in while packing was with a packhorse named Sarge and a pair of elk antlers. We were packing out of our Grizzly Creek camp up over Wallace to Mill Creek one day and I was the tail-end Charlie with the tail-end pack string. I had four colts and Sarge.

Sarge might as well have been a colt; he was ornery as they come and always leading the packhorses off or the saddle horses off. Kind of a contrary son of a gun yet he was nice to have around.

I was about halfway up to Wallace and I saw a set of elk antlers leaning against a tree with a note on it. One of our clients from Arizona found a winterkill elk and he wanted me to pack

56

the antlers out. Since he was a pretty good client and had been with us several times I thought, "Well why not, I'll try."

I had all manty packs which are side packs and not very conducive to packing elk antlers. I didn't have any rope or tarp or anything else to tie them down with so I had to use the end of some of my sling ropes and a few things like that. I got them all tied down on Sarge and was headed up the trail.

It lasted about 100 yards until he shook them loose and they were popping them in the rear end. He didn't like that very good. So I stopped and I redid them. That might have gone 200 yards and it kind of went that way for quite a while.

I finally got up to about Wallace Pass and the points started sticking old Sarge in the rear end. Boy, he was going around the packhorses creating quite a mess. I finally got the packhorses anchored to a tree and Sarge is still going around them raising hell.

So I thought, well I'd better anchor him. I untied him; there was a tree right handy. Before I could get him tied to a tree he took off dragging me and the elk antlers. Pretty quick a manty came off and soon we're going around in a circle. I look down and there's a rope about ready to wind me up. I knew if I ever got wound up in that rope that was tied to his packsaddle I was a dead man. So I did a little exhibition work and high jumping and fast footing, things like that and got out of danger.

About that time he pulled the halter rope loose. Well, that horse went down through the draw, hell bent for election. The last I saw of him he was still dragging one pack and an elk antler. I jumped on my saddle horse and took after him. I can hear him crashing down through there. I thought, well, hell this will be easy. Pretty quick I don't hear anything. I do find one side of the elk rack and all of the duffel.

So I started looking for Sarge. And I rode up and down and crossways in that draw. Couldn't find Sarge.

After a while my wife and Kenny Barnes got worried about me and came looking. So we all three looked for that horse and we still didn't find him. Finally Kenny says, "Well, you guys have to get those dudes taken care of, I'll go back and keep looking. I'll ride back to camp, maybe he went down there. I'll stay all night and then come out tomorrow."

Well, he looked again the next day, and he came out. He didn't see him.

We scoured Mill Creek. I flew for the little son of a gun, still couldn't find him. One week went by, pretty quick two weeks was gone, then three weeks was gone. Then it's time to go hunting. So when we went in on the 13th of September, that's about four weeks, got to the top and I handed my pack string to one of the guides.

I says, "I'm going to go take one last look for Sarge."

I rode over to Knife Creek, thought maybe he's holed up there somewhere. I went down Knife Creek and just before I got to Grizzly Creek I met a neighbor from down in the valley.

He says, "Say, did you lose a horse?"

"Yeah, where's he at?"

"Well, he's down there at the creek. We took the packsaddle off. He was a little hard to catch." Apparently he got loose from them.

So I rode down there and sure enough, there's that Sarge. He's just wilder than a March hare. I got around him and finally head him for Grizzly Creek. He cut out of there on a dead run and probably beat me to camp by about two hours.

Anyway, I get to camp and here he is out in the meadow blowing and snorting and finally he ran into the corral and he's standing there wild-eyed. We finally get him caught. He's pretty dinged up but nothing deep or serious. So I took him home and turned him out to pasture for a month and he was okay. We decided we might as well sell him as he was always getting in some kind of trouble.

That was probably the most dangerous situation I've been in while packing. Had that rope got me and I started to drag, I probably wouldn't be here to tell this.

Make Sure He Bucks Before You Ride Him

We bought a paint horse, a big paint gelding, last year from a gal about 70 years old. Saw it advertised in the paper or heard about it being for sale or something. We called her up, "Yeah, it's for sale". She had a price on it.

So we went and took a look at it. Kind of liked it. Finally before we bought it she says, "There is one problem with that horse, he bucks with a saddle on". He's never bucked with a rider that she knew of but he bucked when you saddled him up.

Well, I didn't think that'd be too much problem as she probably didn't ever ride him but once a year, maybe twice a year. As much as we rode, why, we'd take that right out of him.

Well, the first time I rode him, I tied him up to the horse trailer and pulled the cinch up and he proceeded to buck, but he didn't move his hind feet. He was really making waves though, he thought. So we rode him a year, even put dudes on him. I'd just tell them, "Make sure you don't crawl on him until he's bucked."

The second year I rode him up Big Creek right after he was in off grass. Saddled him up, didn't think much about him, you know, he'd quit bucking the year before towards the end of the season.

"Well heck, he's all broke this year." He didn't buck.

I get on him, head up the trail and, "Whoops", he says, "I forgot to buck". And he proceeds to buck, or try to, with me holding on the reins and pulling him back.

Well, we went up the trail about halfway to camp and something happened. He decided "Well, I didn't get to buck back there, guess I'll buck up here". So he tried her again.

That horse had been over the trail, probably had 100 miles on him now, up over Wallace Pass. I think he's kind of given up the bucking now maybe for this year, I hope.

Watch the Hooves

I've been kicked by horses a few times. I was in Slough Creek one time packing up. We had an old packhorse named Ugly. I was getting ready to pack him up and I cinched him up. Then I started around to the offside to see that everything was right. Ol' Ugly cut loose and got me pretty good with both hind legs with his hocks. It didn't really pop, it just went ump.

He picked me up and threw me about ten feet. I laid there for a while. The main thing that was wrong was that I had the wind knocked out of me. Finally got up and finished packing the old son-of-a-gun. Far as I know that's the only time Ugly ever kicked.

One of our guides was out one day helping me catch some horses. Had a two-year-old colt named Scotch in the bunch. We had them crowded up in a little catch pin. Stan reached out and put his hand on Scotch's rump. Scotch let fly with both hind feet and caught Stan just above the knees. I wasn't the one that was kicked but I know about how hard it hurt. Stan rolled under the fence and laid there for quite a while before he started navigating again.

That first string of mules I told you about, we had them in the stalls up in a barn in Cooke City one day right after we got them. I grabbed Rosie's packsaddle and started to walk in the stall with her and she cut loose with both hind feet and caught the packsaddle. That took most of the blow, but it still knocked me clear across the alleyway in the barn. I'm glad I had that packsaddle to kind of shield myself with.

I was coming down from chasing horses off of Woody

Basin one time and the saddle horse I was riding was going like hell down there, I made the mistake of trying to guide him. There was a big tree coming up and it looked like he was going on one side. I decided I wanted him to go on the other side. He just missed the tree with himself but he ran my leg into the tree.

Of course, that all swelled up about twice as big as it should have been and turned black. So I went and got an x-ray on it and they says, "No it ain't broke."

I hobbled around a long time with that thing until it finally healed up. About ten years later, I had to go and get an x-ray on it again for some reason or other. The doc, he was reading the x-ray and he says, "When did you break this leg?"

"I never did break that leg."

"Oh, yes you did," he says, "look at this." Sure enough, it had been broke.

That's about all the times I've been kicked in all my years of working with animals and I've worked with quite a few different animals as we usually run 30-80 head of horses.

Blue & Scrooge

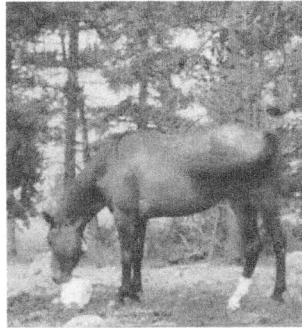
Ginger, Sonya's mare

We are presently about halfway to our Grizzly Creek camp. As this is the first trip of the year there are a lot trees across the trail we have had to cut out. This is a real nice camp located at the lower end of Grizzly Meadows and sits up on a rocky point which stays pretty warm. There is a meadow about a mile and a half long with good feed for the horses.

You wouldn't think horses and mules would leave this camp with all the good feed that is available but they still get the urge to roam. I have chased horses various directions that have left this meadow.

The Grass is Always Greener on the
Other Side of the Mountain.

This is a tale about horses gone astray

I was camped on Slough Creek at our Bull Creek camp one summer trip. Had about six or eight dudes and the cook, Shelly, Danny Mills, and myself. Danny went to wrangle the horses one evening and he came back and says, "I think they're headed for Buffalo, I think they went up the trail."

So I jumped on my horse and after them we went. We got down to the Buffalo camp and sure enough there they stood in the campsite. I told Danny, "You go back up the trail heading for Hellroaring and I'll head them up, you head them back towards Slough Creek. Don't let them get past you." When I got back up there towards the Ranger Station here's Danny.

He explained "They just run right over the top of me, I

couldn't stop them."

So I headed up the trail towards Hellroaring and caught the horses several times but couldn't get ahead of them on the switchback or anything. I figured, well, we're going to have to catch horses in the corrals at Grizzly Creek. We got up on top and I lost track of them so I started down the other side.

There was one damn mule that came up behind me, I figured it got lost or something, was trying to catch up to the other horses. Well, I couldn't catch it, couldn't get it turned. So I went back up on top and thought, I don't think these horses went over the top. We're just going to stay here. We slept there all night the best we could.

Craig Neal, nephew

The next morning I got to investigating and sure enough, there's a trail going north up the divide. I went up there a ways and yep, there's the horses. So I headed them back the way we came. Danny headed them down into Buffalo. We kept them going hard enough that when we got down to Buffalo they went straight across instead of heading down country to the old camp.

We got back into our camp in Slough Creek about 9:00 that morning. Quite an ordeal wrangling horses about 12-14 hours.

The reason the horses had jumped the trail up on Hummingbird instead of going over the top is Boy Scouts had been there about a week before and had put up a new monument there alongside the trail which spooked the horses. If it hadn't been for that we would have been wrangling horses in the corral there at Grizzly Creek I'm quite sure of it.

One time I lost some horses and finally found them on the bridge at Emigrant. Ruth and I cornered them there, opened the gate on the horse trailer and loaded them right there on the bridge. It's amazing how good a corral a bridge will make.

They've gone out to the trailhead several times and hung around there waiting for us to come and get them or maybe they were waiting for someone to come along and open the door on the horse trailers and give them a ride home. A time or two they've gone up Knife Creek.

Horse Stealing

Now, you heard about horse stealing in the Old West. Well I can't prove who did it, how it was done or anything else, but I'm positive we had some horses stole every fall when we were in Cooke City. We had some horse pasture up in Woody Basin, and every fall when we'd go to get our horses suddenly some would disappear. It might be one, or two, or three, or four. I think four was the most.

You could ride for a week at a time, two or three guys, in all directions, never find the horses. It was always horses easy to catch too. Two or three weeks later, lo and behold, here the horses would show up back in the pasture.

I didn't have a thought as to what was going on for quite a while, but finally one of my wranglers left his mother's horse with ours up at Cooke City for a couple days until we could get my horses moved back. Lo and behold, her horse disappeared. But when it returned it had a big old wither sore on it. It had been used. I assume somebody had been going hunting or just sightseeing with our horses and didn't want to rent them. I had

69

my suspicions about where they went, but I don't know for sure.

We had another horse just about stole, actually it wasn't our horse, it belonged to a friend of ours, Mike Warren. The horses took off on us from Slough Creek camp and we got them all turned back but Mike's horse, up on top of the pass going into Buffalo Forks. We had to move camp over to Buffalo Fork later. Rode past there the next day and nothing happened.

Ruth and I rode up there the next day after that. We still didn't see the horse. We went down the ridge a little ways, back into our camp on Buffalo. So we moved on over to Grizzly Creek in a couple days, still don't have the horse. I had to bring that trip out as Stan, one of our guides, was in Grizzly Creek with another trip.

After I get out, Vern Smith called wanting to know if we were short a horse. I said we were. Well, his guides had seen a guy trying to catch a horse of that description, and in fact he did catch a horse. He took it to his camp, then apparently got cold feet and headed the horse up toward Grizzly Creek.

Now how the horse found his way back into our camp, we are not sure. He had never been over the trail from where he had been captured by the horse thieves, to our camp, that we know of.

Another strange thing that's happened with our horses was in the Daily Lake pasture. It's got great big boulders in there, about half the size of a truck or something like that. Horses would get up against this boulder to switch flies and get in the shade and things.

One year I went up to wrangle the horses and found Ruth's private horse and one mule had big ol' rake marks down their sides. Pretty sure it was mountain lion. And I assume they was laid up on the boulders and waited till the horses come along and jump on them. They never did hurt a horse very bad, but they sure raked them up.

The first year we outfitted we didn't have quite enough horses for hunting season so I borrowed a few from a good friend of ours, people that owned Chico Hot Springs at that time. Used them all season and everything went hunky dory, all the horses stayed there until the last night we were up there.

We were getting ready to pull camp the next morning, wrangled the horses but we didn't have one of the Chico horses, kind of a dark chestnut mare. We looked and looked and looked for that mare, we never did find her.

I finally paid Chico for the horse. Several years later we found horse bones clear up on top of the ridge which were

71

probably hers. The horse had never been over the trail to get up there but it's the only thing I could explain of her disappearance.

Lost Horse

This year we're back in Grizzly Creek hunting and one of the dudes tied his horse up, or forgot to tie him up maybe would be a better word. We come back from hunting and his horse was gone. We rode all over half of Hellroaring a couple of three days and never did find the horse so we packed up and come out finally. Jim says, "I'll be flying again, I'll look for him." The next day he flew and he found the horse.

So we rode in and got this horse found and caught and decide well, we'll come down this Passage Creek which was supposed to be cleared. This crew may or may not have been up Passage Creek in 20 years but the trail was not good. We finally did make it out. We lost the trail about halfway down and were in bogs and down timber and stuff like that for quite a ways.

Don't ever believe a Forest Service individual when they say they cleared a trail unless they're using a chainsaw.

Those Durn Bears!

I guess we'll talk about bears for a while.
In Grizzly Creek camp we used to hang all our food in a tree
when we left. Finally a bear got up on the meat pole and got
some food out of the cooler we had hanging up there. Well that's
all it took. Pretty quick we had bears in the morning, bears in the
night, bears at noon, bears at midnight. You name it, we had
bears.

One of my guides told me he went outside once in the
middle of the night and he says there was seven bears on the
meat pole. I don't know if that many bears could get on that meat
pole but there must have been a bunch.

We finally started taking a dog into camp and after that

we never had any more bear problems until a government agent opened one of our storage barrels we leave stuff in all winter. Somebody had to get smart and snoop. I don't know if he deliberately left it open or whether he didn't shut it good. Anyway, a bear got into it and so then we had more bear problems. That was in about 1978.

Elmer

We had a cook named Elmer. He had probably one tooth in his head. He was a good cook. Worked for us off and on for two or three years. Then he wouldn't show up for work. He had a little bit of a problem with bars and booze and stuff like that. But he was a good cook, even wore a white apron and chef's cap. He had a butcher knife that must have had a two-foot blade.

"What you need that for?" I ask.

"Well," he says, "to protect me from the bears. It isn't to kill the bears, it's to cut a hole in the back of the tent so I can get out of here!"

Luckily, he didn't ever have to cut a hole in the back of the tent.

Frenchy

JOSEPH (FRENCHY) B. DURET
NATIVE OF FRANCE

PIONEER, PARK COUNTY TRAIL BLAZER AND NATIONALLY KNOWN HUNTER, TRAPPER AND GUIDE, LOST HIS LIFE IN HAND-TO-HAND ENCOUNTER WITH A HUGE GRIZZLY BEAR ON JUNE 12, 1922.

WHEN DURET TRIED TO DISPATCH THE TRAPPED BEAR WITH A BULLET WHICH EVIDENTLY DID NOT REACH A VITAL SPOT, THE ENRAGED ANIMAL BROKE THE CHAIN WHICH HELD THE TRAP PIECES OF GRIZZLY FUR, STRANDS OF HAIR, TORN BITS OF FLESH, THE BLOOD SOAKED GROUND, AND CHEWED RIFLE STOCK ALL BORE MUTE TESTIMONY TO THE STRUGGLE THAT ENSUED.

MR. DURET'S BODY WAS FOUND NEAR THIS SPOT ON JUNE 13. ON JUNE 15, ASST. BUFFALO KEEPER HUTCHINS AND RANGER DEMINOFF, BOTH OF YELLOWSTONE PARK, BURIED THE BODY AND READ OVER IT SOME VERSES FROM THE BIBLE AND SAID A PRAYER.

MR. DURET WAS A FRIEND OF THEODORE ROOSEVELT WHOM HE CONDUCTED ON SEVERAL HUNTING AND FISHING TRIPS IN THIS AREA.

GALLATIN NATIONAL FOREST

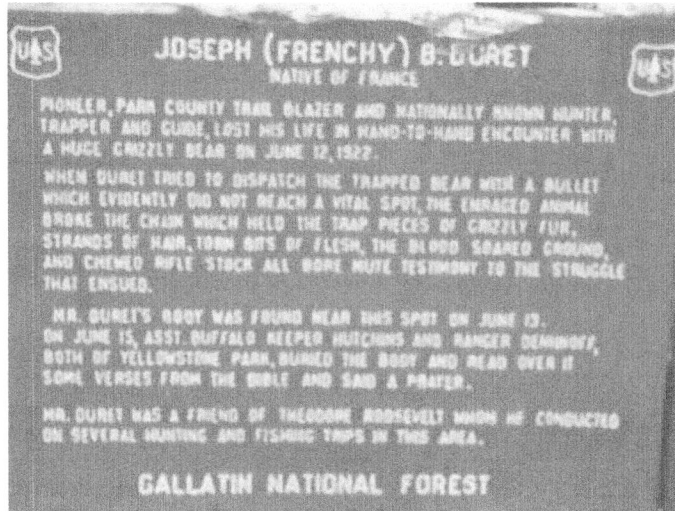

Now we're camped on Slough Creek just below Frenchy's Meadow so I'll tell you a tale about Frenchy Dureau.

He was an emigrant from France that came over to this country to be a mountain man, explorer, trapper, you name it. He guided Teddy Roosevelt many times. Teddy is supposed to have made sure that Frenchy could get a homestead on Slough Creek.

75

Pierce family

Frenchy put up hay on his homestead and hauled it up to Cooke City to feed the horses where at the time there was supposed to have been 1,000 to 1,200 head of horses wintering.

He trapped grizzly bear, mink, otter, and stuff like that. He probably poached a lot of elk and fed the miners. In 1922 he trapped a grizzly bear. He went out of his cabin one morning to check his traps and never returned.

His wife contacted the ranger down in Yellowstone Park and they started a search for Frenchy and found him not too far below the cabins, or what we left of him. Frenchy had evidently trapped a grizzly and when he went to shoot it the grizzly broke loose and charged him. A very fierce battle ensued. Bits of hair and blood and gore were scattered about. The bear got the best of Frenchy.

A monument to Frenchy has been put up and I often take dudes by it to look at it.

One story I heard was that Frenchy and his wife were having problems and his wife took all the bullets out of his gun but one that morning when he went after the grizzly bear. The trap, I understand, was found on the Yellowstone River and hangs at the present time in the lodge at the Silver Tip.

The Silver Tip ranch owns the property at this time; 700 acres of private property within the bounds of the Absaroka Beartooth Wilderness and Yellowstone Park on the south. The ranch owners and management should be commended for allowing travelers through the area to use the meadows for horse pasture. They've been very generous over the years.

They run their own horses and all the horses that are turned out for about a five-mile stretch of Slough Creek above the park boundary that use Frenchy's Meadow, all private ground. If it was ever fenced it would be very unhandy for both the Silver Tip and the traveler; Silver Tip to get their horses across the Forest Service to the private ground at night then back in the morning, and the traveler to get around Frenchy's Meadow portion of the ranch.

Kick Him in the Nose

We used to take big Wilderness Association trips. I think we had 30 people on one and one of the guests was Aileen Crane and her daughter. When we'd got into Grizzly Creek there had been quite a few bears there.

We got to looking around and told everybody not to pitch their tent on the bear trail; the timber in back of the cook tent. Well, Aileen and her daughter went and pitched their tent right on the bear trail. They had a little teepee, or herder tent.

In the middle of the night, Aileen woke up and she had a little black bear in the tent with her pulling her saddlebags out. She was sleepy and just kicked it in the nose and says, "Get away bear." The bear left and she went back to sleep, slept soundly until morning.

The next morning she got to thinking about it and what had happened. So she told people and it got talked up a little bit. That evening around the campfire it got talked up a little more. Finally the trip director came to me and says, "You know, they're really scared, they don't want to sleep out there tonight."

"Well," I says, "they can move in the wrangler tent if they want to, if they can sleep with all the snoring."

I had told people not to take any food items into their tent, that includes toothpaste and perfume and what have you, and that's why they had a live teddy bear in their tent. Aileen had brought in her saddlebags off of her saddle and she didn't really have any food in there but she did have her empty lunch sack. That was all it took.

Sow and Cubs

I had a summer guest, Tyrone, been here several years, that I took on a pack trip, just the two of us. We went back to Hellroaring and stayed a few days, and then we had a private party trip coming in. We were going to meet Ruth up on the pass and were going on in over into the Basin.

We get up about to the pass and I hear "Woof," and I says to Tyrone, "Do you see that bear?" I couldn't see her.

"Oh yes," he says, "right there." Yes, she was right there, not far either, about 20 or 30 yards. My sister-in-law, Anita, was the cook and a few days before that she had seen a sow and two cubs there. I figured well, this is a sow and two cubs and I don't want to get between them.

So I just froze and held my horse still. The sow come around, keeping her head towards us, her teeth going clack, clack, clack. Finally she moved on around this rock ledge she was up against and took off. So I rode up on top to see where she was going to and here's her cub. That cub was just about as big as she was, both of them were Silvertips. I'm just glad she was in a good disposition that day.

Custer

On the first trip across from Cooke City to Mill Creek we camped on the Langston Meadow on Lake Abundance Creek which is the first meadow up Lake Abundance Creek from Frenchy's Meadow. Claude Custer kind of started this outfit way back in the Fifties and he helped us a lot, usually led the dudes. He was a pretty great guy, had a gift of gab.

He took off with the dudes the morning we were moving to Buffalo Fork. Before he got to Slough Creek he ran into four grizzly bears, a sow and probably three 2-year olds from the way it sounded.

"Well," Custer says, "I told the dudes to about-face and they changed directions just like a bunch of chorus girls. I haven't been able to do that the whole trip." He got them back out of the way and then Custer made a charge on the bears and run them off. Got the dudes started back down the trail and the last guy on the trail, he says he looked up above the trail and there sat another grizzly bear. So I guess there were five grizzly bears that morning.

On that same trip, the first night we got into camp, after we saw that there had been so many bears around we decided we needed someone to guard the food. We had a big ice cream shipping container that we used for a cooler that we put in the ground in front of the cook tent. Custer says, "I'll guard the cooler."

So he rolled his bedroll out with his head up against the cooler and proceeded to go to sleep. The next morning I looked and the cooler is tipped over. There was a ham bone, clean, slicker than a whistle. I thought maybe ol' Custer had got hungry in the middle of the night, but he swore he hadn't. He just didn't wake up when the bear had come in and ate the ham.

The cook was in the cook tent, says "Well, I heard it."

I asked, "Why didn't you yell and wake somebody up?"

"I didn't want it to come in the cook tent and get me!"

Custer guided for me a little bit on summer trips mainly. One year in here hunting, the hill got a little icy over the pass. It's not all that great a pass, it's quite a ways down on one side and pretty much straight down.

We were getting ready to go and I ask Custer, "Custer, are you going to ride down or walk down the pass?"

He says, "I'm going to ride, that horse has got four legs and I only have got two."

So that's what we did, rode over the pass. Just close your eyes, hang on to the saddle horn, and trust your horse. About all you can do sometimes.

Never had anybody slide off of it. We did have some mules slide off it. I finally killed one this year. A boulder on the upper side of the trail flipped over and landed in under him and I don't know just what happened, but anyway, he wound up dead. Luckily, that doesn't happen very often.

Strong Bear

At Grizzly Creek camp we had a 55-gallon barrel buried in the cook tent. Well, one day we rode into camp and there's the barrel, just beat all to pieces. A bear had banged it on rocks and dented it but never did get it open, but he sure busted every piece of glass that was inside that barrel.

I had a couple of yahoos there that didn't do much work so I put one of them to burying that barrel. Two or three days later I decided I'll go up there and see what happened up there where the barrel was buried. I figured the grizzly had dug it out of the ground.

No, that wasn't the case. The grizzly just grabbed a'hold of it and pulled it straight up out of the ground, no digging involved. That shows how strong a grizzly bear is.

We use that barrel for food storage when we're gone, it's bear-proof. It's done a great job so far and about 30 years a bear has never got one of them open. We used to put food on the meat pole back there and when we were gone, hang it. Black bears came into camp and the cubs climbed up the tree, out on the pole, and down the rope, and throw all the food out of the manty or whatever we had it in, down to mama.

We could come in and see a manty hanging there and

think boy, everything is okay today, until you got right up to it, and there wasn't anything left in the manty.

To Hang or Not to Hang?

In the early Eighties a friend of ours sold his outfitting business along the park line in Buffalo Forks to a younger person who did not have much experience in the business. He wanted to be an outfitter and tried extremely hard.

The Forest Service decided everybody had to have a meat pole 100 yards from camp to hang their food. They come in to our camp and told me that and I said I wouldn't do it because it was nothing but a bear attractant. We had had a lot of problems over the years with food hung on meat poles, so to speak.

I says, "If I have one I want it right in camp."

The new outfitter wanted to get along with the Forest Service so he went out in the woods 100 yards from camp and he built a meat pole. He put some pellets on it and a few other things.

The first night it was up, a black bear came into camp and climbed a tree and got the pellets down. There had been a grizzly bear waltzing by that camp for about 18 years and he hadn't bothered anything; all food smells were mixed with human smells too. But this black bear gets things down and the grizzly decides somebody is getting something to eat.

So the grizzly ran down and chases the black bear off and eats up the pellets and then waltzes on into camp. It scared everybody in camp half to death and so they called the Forest Service. A day or so later here come two people from the Forest Service and they're going to solve the problem. They tied a snare to a big tree and left. The grizzly bear comes in and sticks his foot in the snare, must have been a hind foot.

You've all heard that grizzly bears do not climb trees. I don't know whether or not he climbed the tree but there wasn't any bark left on that tree for about 30 feet in the air so I guess he did. And he also got away.

So the powers that be decided they'd use a culvert trap. They went in and they set it right in front of the cook tent. They were having a little trouble getting the bear to go in it to catch it. The problem was a guide in the camp was going in at night springing the trap and sleeping in the trap at night so the bear couldn't get him. So eventually they did capture the bear.

The young outfitter was a little disturbed. I went down there and he says yes, they captured it, tranquilized it, checked its teeth, collared it, and they turned it loose. Then they gave the guys in camp a radio directional deal to tell them where the bear was. They weren't too sure whether that radio deal was working, if they couldn't find the bear or not, so they assumed the bear was right in camp with them.

At that same camp later the cook was walking out to the Transfer and walked up on a grizzly that wooled her around a little bit, but she survived the experience.

Bandit Bear

Sonya & Shawna

In Big Creek we had a problem with a bear one time.

A hunter killed a spike bull and we had it hanging on the meat pole in back of camp. The rack, if you call a spike a rack, was lying there on the ground by the tree.

One day at noon we came into camp and saw a bear going up the hill. We went out and checked the meat, the meat's okay. But the hunter didn't check the meat, he checked the rack. There isn't any. Boy, was he mad. Bear had got away with his big rack!

So I went looking, there was enough snow to trail the

bear. I finally found the elk rack. He had taken it back behind a tree and covered it up. Didn't have to use much duff to cover it, I'll tell you. That bear kept coming back. The hunters kind of wanted a bear but they never did get a chance at him.

Finally one night I stepped out of the tent and I heard him back there shinnying. He usually ran off but he's going up the tree this time to sit. I grabbed my rifle and threw it up and shot him. He's mounted on my wall right now and he's a pretty good trophy, measured six feet. He's the only bear I've shot, the only bear I've ever felt like shooting.

Bear Experts

Over in Slough Creek one time we run into a bear biologist. He had a bear trap in there and he was studying these bears. He knew all about bears, according to him. He was working for the Knight people.

We invited him up to camp one night and he was telling us how great a bear trapper he was. He could burn a little honey down there in that culvert trap he had and he'd catch all the bears within five miles. We were there for about three or four more days and he never caught a bear. There were fresh tracks every morning right by his trap in Slough Creek.

I asked him, "How do you tell grizzly scat from black bear scat?"

"The grizzly scat is 2¼" in diameter and the black bear's is smaller than that," so he says.

I says, "Well, you can have big black bears and you also have little grizzlies."

"No," he says, "that's the way it is. The grizzly is all 2¼" and the black bear is smaller than that."

Well, I didn't argue with them; he was the bear biologist.

On that same trip when we got over to Hellroaring we met another bear biologist. They were all with the Inner Agency Bear Study Team about the first year it started up. He'd been from Wallace and clear down to Grizzly Creek to Hellroaring. I says, "Did you see any bear sign?"

"Oh, yeah, eight sightings."

I says, "You mean black bear."

"No, grizzly."

I'm sure there hadn't been a grizzly up Grizzly Creek, at least not more than one in about ten years.

In a couple of days we went up Grizzly Creek. We were the first ones over the trail since the biologists had walked down it. Sure enough, there's a bear track on the trail right off the bat. Little black bear, probably a two-year-old. We'd go a little ways and the bear would wander off in the timber. After a while, here was the bear back on the trail. For sure the same bear, he didn't get any bigger or smaller.

We did that all the way to Wallace. By the time we got to the top up that bear had hit the trail eight times. So I suppose that was the eight bear sightings the biologists had made.

So that's the story of bears. Most people are scared to death of them. They do have to be respected but I think more problems are created through fear than anything unless it'd be over-confidence.

A Hunting We Go

Craig

In 1972 Russell Broughton and his son, Stan, booked a hunt out of our Upper Bark Cabin spike camp. Opening morning Stan got a six-point bull elk in Cottonwood Creek. They called me on the radio to bring mules up to pack the thing out.

Had to go up on top of the divide and back out of Bark Cabin Creek and back down to their elk. The snow was pretty deep on top but I heard that somebody had cut the trail out down Cottonwood Creek. Now, this trail hadn't been cleared for probably 40 or 50 years but I figured well, if they cut it out maybe it would be okay to pack down it.

So I headed down with the elk instead of back over the top, which was a big mistake. There were bogs, the trail had slid out, there were trees across the trail. It wasn't in good shape but

I finally made it down. I dumped my elk on a rock and went back to camp and had supper. After that I had a rule - no one was to go into Cottonwood Creek unless you could get a mule over the top both ways. Since 1972 I've never been down that trail again and I don't intend to go. I have gotten quite a few elk out of Cottonwood but they've all come out over the top.

Just Close Your Eyes and Trust Your Horse

Twenty years ago we were back in Hellroaring hunting. In the meantime two guys showed up at Pray and they wanted to go in and go fishing. So Ruth called a friend of ours up and asked him if he could take them in. Sure, he could take them in. So they go up Mill Creek and back up over Wallace, down to camp. I'm leaving the next day to bring the hunters out so I didn't really get to meet these guys very long.

But one of the things one of the guys says to me is, "Is there another way out of here other than over Wallace?" Didn't care much for Wallace Pass, I guess.

I says, "Well, no, not really. Any other way and you're going to be a long ways from home when you get out."

So we leave and the next morning they made the guide pack up and go down through Yellowstone Park. The guide had never been down over this trail and I don't think he knew the swinging bridge was there either. He was pretty upset as they'd only stayed overnight and they were supposed to have been staying four or five days, something like that. They had to camp one night down at the park line.

They were riding out across the flats just this side of Tower Junction and when you come around a little bend in the trail here's the swinging bridge, right there. He just put the spurs to his horse and put him on. Of course, the dude's horses followed and went right on. They're gawking around and they get out in the middle of the bridge and it starts going like this, up and down, swaying and stuff like that. About scared them half to death, they thought they were in an earthquake.

They get on up to the road which is up on the top of the hill not very far, unsaddle, and they're 60 miles from home. So the guide had to hitchhike out to Tower to a telephone to call Ruth to bring a horse trailer down there. He left them guys sitting on their duffel up there at the parking lot. I think it was getting pretty dark by this time. Them guys, I think, wished they went back over Wallace.

Lunar Hunting

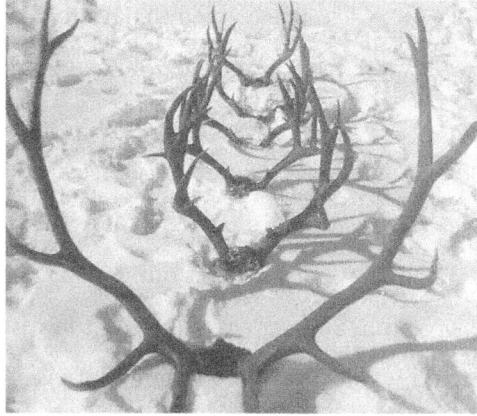

We were up Big Creek hunting one fall, the first hunt in late October. We had a bunch of guys from Florida, there were four of them and I was guiding two of them. The other two were guided by somebody else. One guy took a fishing pole but Big Creek isn't all that good fishing especially in October. Not much creek to fish. But he wanted to fish.

On the third evening Davy Crocket Jones told me, "In the morning we're just going out to hunt the major. Then we're coming back and I'm going to go fishing."

I says, "What in the hell's the major?"

"Well," he says, "the signs of the moon. The only time you're going to catch an elk up grazing is during the major or the minor and the major is at 8:00."

"Well," I said, "we can't go very far if we're going to have to be there at 8:00. Then we're going to have to come back. There's a little meadow right back of camp, I'll take you up there."

Davy and his buddy and I got on our horses. Well, we get up there and we're 200 yards from the meadow yet in the scattered timber. My horse sticks his ears out, I stopped, I looked, can't see anything. So I step my horse a little ways farther. Hell, there's a whole bunch of elk right out in the middle of the meadow. And they're looking at us.

I says, "Let's slip on up there."

We went up there and got off our horses. I got him out to the edge of the trees and looked around for his buddy. His buddy was back there about 200 yards like he usually is. It was just light enough that you could see pretty good. I get my glasses out and these elk are milling.

Finally I say, "Well that one's coming around and right there's a bull."

Bang! The ol' hair flew off that son-of-a-gun. Nothing happened, they just kept milling. They went up the mountain a little ways but they stayed out in the middle of the meadow. I says, "Here he comes again."

Kebang! They go down the meadow a little farther. Every time they milled, they went up the mountain a little about the length of the mill. There was probably a dozen head of cows and one bull. That went on. He shot five times. He was hitting the bull every time he came around.

Finally I decided I better go get my rifle. The other guy had got there by then. They're still shooting. There's timber within 75 yards on three sides of him, the only side there wasn't any timber was behind him, the way they went. They were always within 75 yards of timber on two sides of him all the time they were shooting.

I almost get back from retrieving my rifle and the elk had just about went over the top. I heard Davy Crockett Jones say, "He's standing right by that tree." He shot once more and that son-of-a-gun come rolling down the mountain. Then everything busted loose and they all left.

We went up there and drug that son-of-a-gun down where we could gut him out. They wanted to skin him so I started skinning him. He had two shots through the lungs, one through the heart, one had hit him on the head, one hit him on the leg. He had a hole in one ear, and two or three holes in the antlers.

I think they'd hit him damn near every time they shot, which was about 12 or 14 shots.

That elk just wouldn't drop! He went clear to the top of that mountain and still didn't drop. The one that did drop him finally was the heart shot, it was the one that rolled him out of there.

I started keeping track that year and of all the elk we killed, 70 percent of them was killed during the major or the minor. That kind of made a believer out of me there's something to that lunar stuff.

Who Was Supposed to Bring the Gun?

Mariah

The first year we outfitted we went into the Gallatin the first of October and had two 10-day hunts over there. Then we'd move back over the top into Big Creek for the general season. In the Gallatin there were always grizzly bear tracks around. You'd get a fresh snow, ride a circle and you'd see two or three different bear tracks.

Some hunters we had in the drop camp down on Porcupine came up one night the first week of the season. They say, "We need some elk packed out in the morning, we got three of them."

I says, "Okay, where are they?"

He kind of told me and says, "We'll meet you there on the trail and take you up to the elk. If I can have a horse I'll ride out with them to get it processed." So we made plans accordingly.

I and a guide or two went down to the meeting place, the rest of the help in the main camp went hunting with the hunters that we had. We got down to where the elk were, in real thick dog-haired Lodgepole Pine thicket. I looked at it and decided well, that really wasn't any place for my saddle horse. So I tied him up to the trail. I told the rest of them, "You might as well tie your horse at the trail." I left my rifle there too, for I didn't figure I needed it. I guess everybody else left their rifles, too, except for one guy, luckily.

Sure enough, there were three elk. The guys had drug them down to a little opening about the size of our cook tent and they were laying on a rock. About that time I heard a hell of a roaring and commotion up the hill a little ways.

It's a grizzly. He's on the gut pile and is raising hell. He's afraid we're going to come up there and take his gut pile, I guess, which we weren't about to.

I looked around the clearing to see who had a rifle. Lo and behold, nobody had a rifle but one guy. I think he was probably the guy that shot all the elk. I wouldn't say for sure, they didn't admit it.

I grabbed him and says, "You sit over here on this rock and you keep watch for that bear. If he comes in, shoot him." That was when everybody had a license, practically, for a grizzly bear. "The rest of us," I says, "we're going to pack these elk up".

It didn't take us very long to get 12 quarters of elk on six horses and get the hell out of there! Of course, we had a little incentive.

Learn the Cold Way

One year we had three hunters from Oregon. There were two of them that were brothers and then a friend. The first day I took them to the head of Bark Cabin and over the top to the head of Cottonwood. We hadn't seen anything and along towards evening we kind of split up and I went with the one brother. The other brother and his friend went in another area. I told everybody to be back at a certain time.

About the time we were supposed to be back the brother I had with me didn't show up. I got a little nervous because it was a long way from camp and it was getting dark, first day the hunters had been in the woods. So I go and look and found him and got him on his horse. The other two guys are sitting up there on top watching all this commotion, probably laughing about it.

The next night Stan took him up back of the main camp. He told him, "Be back at your horse at dark or before dark."

Sure enough, Sam and his friend were at the horses at dark, but no brother. They fired shots and they did this and they did that but they couldn't raise their brother. Finally they came down to camp thinking maybe he's down at camp. No, no brother. Eventually we got an answer on the signal.

Stan went up and dug him out of the jungle on the south side of Big Creek at about midnight. So the next night they went out and did the same thing. They came back to their horses and no brother. So they came back to camp and we discussed what to do.

Sam says, "Well, leave him up there. I've been dragging him out of the woods all my life. It's warm. It will do him good to sit up there."

So sure enough, that's what we did. We couldn't raise a signal shot from him anyway. About 10:00 the next day here he comes stumbling down the creek, through the jungle and into camp. Everybody came in about noon, a little after noon, and decided well, we'll go hunting again.

"Do you want to go, brother?"

Sure, he wanted to go, he was game for it. So they went up and when they came back to the horses, guess what? The brother's sitting there.

John

We had a guy named John from Long Island, New York come out for several years to help around camp up Big Creek. He hunted quite a few years and never killed an elk, he hunted a few more years with us and never killed an elk. But he finally connected. This is the story of the first elk he killed.

We have a place called The Barren, a big meadow that comes down. It's pretty steep coming down but at the end of it there's cliffs, a straight drop. Well, John went up there and he peeked out early one morning and lo and behold, there's a spike bull waiting to be shot. So John lowered the boom on the bull and he dropped and kicked a little bit and he started to fly. John was standing by a tree directly below him. The bull, he flied right by him and John starts to grab him and he thinks, well if I don't stop him I'm going over the edge, too. Now the edge wasn't very far away.

I'm over across the meadow with some hunters and started hearing, boom, boom, boom. After a while I hear boom,

102

boom, boom. Well, I knew it had to be John. You're on your own, John. That's elk hunting.

I come into camp that evening, heard of how the bull had gone over the edge. John had been firing signal shots trying to get some help but nobody came and helped. He did get the bull dressed out and then came on into camp.

He's a Trooper

I've got another story about cold water and hunters. We were in our Big Creek camp one fall hunting elk. We had a camp full of hunters that were all from the same place. One morning about four of them, myself, and a guide decided to walk. It was colder than the devil and I really didn't want to ride on the back of a horse.

When we got down to the creek in front of the camp the only way to get across the creek at that time was to walk a log. I turned to them before I stepped on the log and says "Okay, just one person on the log at a time and you should be okay. If you fall you could grab the log and keep from hitting the water, really."

It's kind of a fast stretch of creek there and it wasn't frozen completely over. I got across and when the last guy was coming across I heard a umpf. I look back and he's in the water. He got up and I says, "You okay?" He didn't say much.

"You okay?" I say again.

Finally he says, "I, I, I think so." He crawled out on the camp side and went back and changed clothes. I'll be darned if he didn't come and catch up to go hunting with us that morning.

Wet Hunter

We had a great big guy in camp one time, must have weighed 300 pounds. The first morning he says, "All I want you guys to do is show me a good place to sit." So Stan took him up on the ridge south of the camp towards Rock Creek, got him up there and came back to camp. The guy carried a great big backpack all the time. I asked him, "What's the backpack for?"

He says, "When I go hunting I like to take off and never stop till I get there and by that time I'm so sweaty and wet that I can't sit down and stay put. So I strip down to nothing, dry off and put on some dry clothes. Then I can sit all day." And he did, for a week.

19 Steps From the Cook-Tent Moose

We had an outfitter friend at several conventions.

One year he says, "I'm going to put in for a moose and goat permit down in your area. If I get the permits can I come down and hunt out of your camp?"

I says, "Yeah, you can do that." There's no way he's going to get a moose and goat permit both, and probably not either one. So I'm pretty safe there.

He'd been a licensed outfitter for umpteen years down in Colorado, and been licensed in Montana for the about the same length of time. That gave him about 30 years of outfitting experience. I figured, boy, this guy knows a lot and I'll learn a lot from him if he comes down.

He decided to come down on a summer trip to scout the area ahead of time for hunting. So that was fine. We went across on the traveling trip to Cooke City.

Pete talked a lot. But we didn't seem to get too much done. He handled the dudes mainly, brushed his horse a lot. He didn't get too many saddled, stuff like that, but we kind of overlooked it. Come hunting season, Pete came down ready to go into camp. Of course, he's telling me how to do things and how I should run the camp and everything. That really didn't go too good.

We had a nationally famous writer in that was also a bow hunter. He wanted to get some stories about bow hunting and some pictures about hunting in general. We also had several hunters on that trip. Pete hunted moose for a few days but could never see a moose.

A hunter would come in and say, "Pete, there's a moose over at the lake," or "Pete, there's a moose down at Hellroaring." Pete would jump on his horse and mosey over there. After a while he'd come back, there ain't been a moose there for a month of Sundays. That got a little tiring for these guys all could differentiate between a moose and a figment of your imagination.

One evening they're sitting around the campfire

and one of the guides, Stan, came back up out of the meadow
from picketing a horse and says, "Pete, there's a moose in the
meadow." Pete jumped up and headed for the meadow. We're
watching him go and about that time somebody says, "Well there
he is, over by the cook tent."

Sure enough he'd come up out of the meadow and was
walking past the cook tent. So I sent somebody after Pete to get
him turned around. The moose kept going through camp and got
up on the rockslide. Well, that moose and Pete met right at the
cook tent. Dressed out that moose 19 steps from the cook tent.

Of course, there were lots of picture taking by the
writer and a lot of people helping, guides, hunters, everybody.
Pete was posing for pictures. Wasn't until quite a while

afterwards that we got to thinking about it. Pete never even opened his pocketknife or his hunting knife. He didn't even use it. He got that moose dressed, quartered, and hung up in record time. The only thing Pete did was pull the trigger on his rifle. That was a 19-steps-from-the-cook-tent moose, we called it.

A few days later Pete decided he'd go goat hunting. I asked Adam, the writer, if he wanted to go with Pete and maybe get a story on goat hunting. He says, "Sure."

They went up to Wallace and looked across. Here's a big old billy goat bedded down about two thirds of the way up the mountainside. So they rode down to the bottom, the closest they could get to the billy with horses. Pete hikes up, traverses the hillside and lo and behold, kills his goat. So he grabs it and started dragging it down the mountain. I guess it was kind of a case of who could out-fumble who.

The writer is taking pictures and Pete is posing. Nobody's gutting the goat. Finally I guess it must have been getting ripe for Pete decided he better cut it open. He took his hunting knife out of his belt and had it poised for a dagger thrust through the body cavity through the hair and hide, through the abdominal wall, into the internal organs, until the writer came to his good senses and stopped Pete from making a mess of things. The writer wound up dressing Pete's goat.

We didn't even get a steak off of that moose.

Buffalo Horn Bull Moose

Ruth and I took off one day and went to Buffalo Horn camp with four horses. We were going to stay there all night and come back out just a day before hunting season. We got in there and we got all unpacked and put our packhorses away and decided we'd take a ride.

We went down the trail towards the park and pretty quick I heard a grunting and eventually a bull moose stepped into the trail ahead of us and started swinging his antlers back and forth and so I told Ruth maybe we ought to go back towards camp. So we turned around and the bull moose did the same thing, circled us and stepped onto the trail and cut us off. Did that about three or four times.

I had my rifle and I was about ready to shoot him but I didn't want to unless I had to and eventually we did get by him and went on our ride. Next morning I got up and we had 11 moose in camp; seven cows and four great big old bulls. They were fighting and bellowing around. We didn't have any horses; I had one picketed, one turned loose, one in the corral, one somewhere else, one hobbled. But they were all gone. What do we do?

I was going to walk back to the trailhead five or six miles and get our horses back but just before I did some friends come and tied up near camp and were going to go hunting. I asked them if I could borrow a horse and they said yes. So I went back to get our horses while Ruth sat in the tent and stared down the moose. Needless to say, we packed out that afternoon.

New Isn't Always Better

I had many goat licenses over the years although I did very little hunting for goat. Never seemed to have much time. Finally back in about 1980-1981 my daughter and I both got a goat tag. I told my wife, "I think maybe I better hunt for that goat this year, for I don't think it's going to be quite so easy to get a tag in the future."

So I took my rifle in on the first hunt in Hellroaring. I had just got a brand new scope that Christmas, a Redfield Widefield scope. I knew I was having a little bit of trouble keeping it sighted in.

I had a little time one day and decided well, I'll go goat hunting. Climbed up on the ridge and sure enough, there's a goat. Got a little way from me out on a steep slope. But he shouldn't roll too far, shouldn't drop any. I'll just take a potshot at him; he's only 70 to 80 yards. I pulled down on him. Kebang. Dust flew about ten feet behind the goat.

What the devil's this? I put another round in. Kebang. Dust flew about ten feet in front of the goat. Try it again. I was either in front or behind the goat, all five shots. I don't think I ever got closer than ten feet.

So I hauled my rifle with the brand new fancy scope back home and borrowed my wife's rifle. Went back in the next week and went back up there in the same spot.

Sure enough, there's the same goat. I drilled him with one shot. That's more like it.

Gary

Harvey

We had a hunter named Harvey. He came from North Dakota. He pulled into Livingston the first day of the hunting season and he called Ruth and wanted to go hunting. Ruth said, "Well, we can't take you right now, you'll have to wait a week."

He says, "That's fine, I'll go up to Missoula and see my sister."

So then the next week when he was supposed to be out at the house at 8:00 on Sunday morning he didn't show up. Finally after a couple of hours Ruth had to go into town and get him out of bed, then he come out to the house. I got him signed in and we're about two hours late now. Ready to go, I says, "Harvey, where's your duffel bag?"

"Well, I haven't packed it yet."

I say, "Well, let's get it packed."

He had a camper on the pickup so we went out. He gets in there and I say, "Give me your duffel bag and you throw out what you want to take to camp." He's throwing stuff out, I'm stuffing it in the duffel and pretty quick he threw me a box of shells. I stuck it in the duffel and he said, "Wait a minute, I might need them."

I said, "You aren't going to need them before you get to

113

camp."

So we finally got to the trailhead and got him on a horse. He couldn't make the horse go so one of the other dudes led him. We got about halfway to camp and lo and behold here's a whole bunch of elk right down below. You know who got off his horse, all ready to shoot them and didn't have any shells in his gun? Harvey. When I got into camp he really gave me the devil.

Festus and Joe

One year I had two guys working for me, Festus and Joe.. One evening one of them come in and says, "My hunter got an elk and it's going to be rough getting it."

I says, "Where is it?"

"Well", he says, "it's down over the edge of Smokey Creek in that pass where you come out of Mist Creek. It's on the Smokey Creek side." That is about straight down. But the elk wasn't down there but 20 yards or 30 yards.

I says, "Okay, you two guys go up there and start quartering that elk and I'll bring the pack string. But I'm going to have to go around Smokey to get there so be a'watching for me."

I knew about where it was but knowing them guys it

114

didn't necessarily have to be where they said it was. So I got up there and here's Festus up on the ridge and he had got one elk quarter.

I says, "Well, how come you packed it up by hand?"

"Well," he says, "you can't get the mules down to it."

I looked over the edge and there's the elk.

I says, "Tell you what, that's what we bring chainsaws for. You take this chainsaw and you cut that little tree and that little tree and I'll bring the mules down and we'll load this elk. The only problem, now we have three quarters instead of four to put on two mules."

I got him loaded up and one quarter balanced on top and turned them loose and headed them for the top. The mules beat it up to the ridge and never slipped a bit. Them boys couldn't believe it, but we got that elk out of there.

Al's Dead Elk

We've got a guy that comes hunting with us, been hunting with us for many years. The first year or two he never got an elk. Then he started getting elk and now he's hunted nine years and got nine elk.

One year he took a little hike behind the Big Creek

camp. He's pussyfooting through the timber and he sees an elk lying down. Boy, that's an easy shot. He shoots, the elk is still lying down. Something ain't right. He walks up to it and the elk was dead, he'd been dead for several days.

That was Al's dead elk.

Don't Get Greedy

We had two guys come elk hunting, one was a great big guy and kind of obnoxious, the other was a young kid, a real nice guy. The first morning I took them up on Smokey. We were still on our horses and I looked across the meadow and there was a whole bunch of elk up against the timber on the other side. It was quite a ways across there.

I get them off their horses and says, "You take a good aim." There were four bulls in the bunch. About the time I got them sat down the big bull went back in the timber. The big guy pulls his trigger, overshoots the elk and hits the timber behind him. The elk thought something was after on the backside so they come running right towards us.

The big guy is shooting and shooting and missing and doesn't hit anything. The young guy is shooting and he's hitting a spike bull which I finally had to pull up and put out of its

116

misery. The big guy is a reloading expert and he had convinced the young guy to use a 6.5 rifle that he had souped up the bullets to about 4,500-foot-per-minute.

I went back to see what the big guy got, which was nothing. I says, "Well, the little guy got a spike."

"That's my spike," he says.

I says, "Well, you couldn't even see that spike."

"That's my spike."

Finally I told the little guy, "Let him tag it. You can go out tomorrow and get a decent bull but you take your 30.06 and leave that little peashooter at home."

In the morning I had him go up on the Lower Stock Drive. Pretty quick we hear shooting and he doesn't come in. Later we hear more shooting and he doesn't come in. Getting pretty near dark and here he comes and told me what he had done.

He run into two six-point bulls on the Lower Stock Drive, shot and wounded one. He dove off in the down timber and followed them to the Upper Stock Drive. Caught up with them and shot again. He goes up to dress it out, it isn't the wounded elk, it's the other one. So he dresses that one out and starts following the other one.

117

He goes clear to Mist Creek, about two more miles through the down timber, took a while. He finally quit about dark and come back to camp and told me what he had done. "Last I saw of it was at Mist Creek and he's lying down every once in a while."

I says, "Well, a guide can go with you in the morning and show him where you last saw the elk and within 200 yards you're going to see it. The guide can shoot it and tag it."

We wound up with three elk in two days; two six-points and a little spike.

The big guy, if he hadn't been quite so greedy, might have had a chance on one of them six-points.

The Political Arena

In this next chapter I'll talk a little bit about my experiences in the outfitter political arena.

The first year after we started outfitting a group of individuals came up with a bill that the outfitters in our area didn't like so we called a little meeting. It turned into a pretty big meeting; I think about 200 outfitters showed up at it. We formed what was called Treasure State Outfitters Association. I was elected as one of the Board of Directors on that association. I believe Paul Christensen was the first president.

We had to draft a set of bylaws and all that stuff to get a formal association set up. That made about five different outfitters associations in the state of Montana. That went on about three or four years.

In 1974 I was elected to the presidency of the Treasure State Association and about a week later I went out and talked to the new president of the Montana Outfitters and Guides, which is probably the other largest association in the state of Montana. We felt that things weren't going very good with four or five associations. We'd go to the legislature, one group would propose something and the other group would oppose the same thing. We had to get together.

About a year later we did get a meeting set up where we elected a group to draft a set of constitution bylaws for a new state association and all the existing associations would disband. I was elected to represent the 300 south central Montanans on the committee. It took several meetings but we did get constitutional bylaws drafted.

We presented them to a combined meeting of the outfitters in the state of Montana in Lewistown in May of 1975. I was again elected on the board of that association. Three years later I was elected to be president of that association which office I held for two years.

When I was first elected president I made the statement that I felt one of the things we really needed to do was organize a national association. A representative from the NRA agreed with me and says, "If you want to call a meeting for Salt Lake City, Utah during our annual meeting, NRA would get the meeting place and host the meeting for us." I called the president of the Idaho outfitters, Norm Guthe, and asked him what he thought about it. He says, "Great let's do it."

So we kind of split the western states up the best we could. I invited some of them, he invited others. We held that meeting in Salt Lake City, Utah and the North American

Outfitters was formed. Rod Dody was the first president and I was still serving as President of MOGA. That made quite a little work for one guy, I felt.

After my tour of duty was up I was still on the board of MOGA for a few more years and I was on the board of North American Outfitters a couple more years. 1982, I believe it was, some things came up and we all went to Washington D.C. to straighten a few things out with the Forest Service. Ralph Holman was chairman of the Montana Outfitter Council, CB Rich was President of Montana Outfitters and Guides Association, and I was Chairman of the Forest Service committee and we represented Montana. There were 53 outfitters that wound up in Washington D.C.; about half horse outfitters and half river outfitters. We stated our case and we got a lot of support out of Congress.

The Forest Service decided maybe we should rewrite the regulations concerning outfitters. That took about a year and a half during which I served on that committee. We'd meet in Salt Lake City, generally. There were, I believe, eight outfitters on the committee. New regulations were written but not always abided by the Forest Service. There were administered many cases that were completely out of line with what was agreed verbally in the meetings. Some of the local rangers were pretty put out because they didn't get to write the regulations. They didn't get administered very well. However, after many changes, we are still operating under those same regulations.

After we got that kind of settled I eventually left the board of directors of MOGA. I try to stay away from as many meetings as possible although I still am a member of the Montana Outfitters and Guides. I don't always agree with what they do, however it's the best game in town.

After serving about 20 years in an active capacity with meetings very frequently it seems good to be able to sit back and relax and not have to attend quite so many outfitter meetings. National parks have been calling two or three days' worth of meetings every year. If you attended all the board meetings of MOGA it would probably be another 10 or 12 days a year, plus we have these resource areas which take up about four or five days a year, the Gallatin Combined Resource Area takes another four or five days a year. That's getting to be about 30 days a year out of your life.

You've got to cut the cards somewhere, I guess.

~Duane Neal

That's All He Wrote...

Duane was 80 years old when he went home to be with our Lord, handing the reins over as Head-Gahoonas to his wife Ruth and outfitter Gary Francis.

In 2006 MOGA honored Duane with the "Old Goat Award"

Happy Trails!

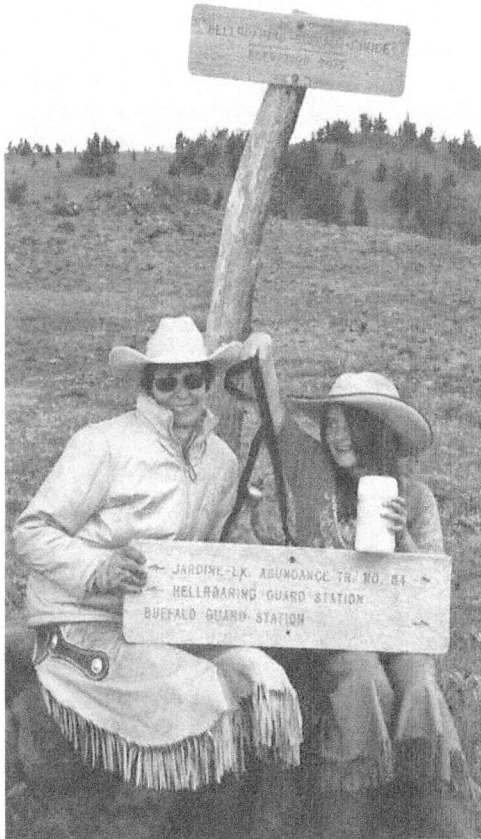

Ruth & Bailey

Whoa Dammit! was published posthumously
as he never got around to publishing it when he was with us.